James on Trials

How Faith Matures in the Storms of Life
James 1:2-25

Carol Ruvolo

Faith at Work
Studies in the Book of James

DEO VOLENTE PUBLISHING

Carol Ruvolo, *James On Trials*

©1997 by Carol Ruvolo.
Published by Deo Volente Publishing
             P.O. Box 4847
             Los Alamos, NM 87544

Cover Design by Patricia Leyba

Printed in the United States of America.

Scripture taken from the NEW AMERICAN STANDARD BIBLE ®, © Copyright The Lockman Foundation 1960, 1962, 1968, 1971, 1973, 1975, 1977, 1995
Used by permission

Appendices A and B are from *Turning on the Light* by Carol Ruvolo. They are used by permission from P & R Publishing.

ISBN: 0-9658804-0-0

James on Trials
How Faith Matures in the Storms of Life

A study that examines the role of trials in strengthening your faith and encourages you to view trials as opportunities to glorify God as your relationship with Him matures.

Endorsements

"Carol Ruvolo has written a new set of Bible lessons for women on the Book of James, focusing on chapter 1 and its teaching about a Christian response to suffering and other trials. The lessons are deeply God-centered, theologically profound and extremely practical. Excellent follow-up questions conclude each lesson to further understanding, promote application, and encourage the student to dig deeper into the Bible."

James Montgomery Boice
Tenth Presbyterian Church

"James on Trials is biblically sound and very practical. It will encourage and challenge both new and maturing believers. I highly recommend it."

Jerry Bridges

"It is exciting to have this book available. Carol Ruvolo gives us right thinking combined with a straightforward manner and Biblical principles that encourage the believer to a lively, God-glorifying faith in all circumstances, especially in our trials."

Vesta Sproul
Ligonier Ministries

"Carol Ruvolo's study is a well-designed tool for getting us to think about what it means to have God's Word in this world of pain and perplexity. Her insistence that we learn to think our thoughts after God and place Him at the center of our lives is a much needed corrective in the life of the Church today."

David F. Wells
Gordon-Conwell Theological Seminary

"Not many published Bible studies manage to be rich in content, easy to use, and practical, all in one package. Here is a refreshing exception. Carol Ruvolo has condensed a tremendous amount of insight into a truly helpful format."

John MacArthur
Grace Ministries

For Patti,

who loves the book of James

Table of Contents

Acknowledgments

This study would never have made it "into print" were it not for the encouragement of the elders at Providence Presbyterian Church in Albuquerque, Randy Steele, Rick Davidson, and John Linebarger; the helpful suggestions from the two women's Bible study groups who labored through the rough draft; my mother, Betty Boling, who kept saying "Of course, you can do this!"; my husband, Frank, and daughter, Cinnamon, who self-sacrificially picked up all the chores I neglected; and the guys at Deo Volente Publishing, Larry Byars, Henry Fernandez, and Mike Inbody, who worked so hard to turn it into a book. My heartfelt thanks to you all!

Carol Ruvolo

Faith at Work
Studies in the Book of James

How to Use this Study Series Effectively

Two books of the Bible have changed my life immeasurably. Paul's letter to the Romans changed the way I think, and James's letter to the twelve tribes dispersed abroad changed the way I live. The two books are very different, but entirely consistent. One is filled with skillfully reasoned theology while the other bulges with wise practical counsel, but the theology and the counsel never clash. They both form part of the necessary bedrock of faith that enables us to walk worthy of our high calling in Christ Jesus.

As you work through these studies, remember you are concentrating on one aspect of faith – faith at work – and like every other part of Scripture, these studies must be understood within the whole counsel of God.

You should also keep in mind that your time is a gift from God to be used in wise stewardship to accomplish His purposes. Paul advised the Ephesians to make the most of their time because the days are evil, and his words apply to us as well (Ephesians 5:15-17). As you undertake these studies, knowing the following information will help you do that.

Know why you are studying.

The Westminster Shorter Catechism asks the question, "What is the chief end of man?" and answers it by saying, "Man's chief end is to glorify God and to enjoy Him forever." (1 Corinthians 10:31; Psalm 73:25-26)[1]

Most of the Christians I know are familiar with that question and answer – even those who have never read the Westminster Confession of Faith or the Catechisms derived from it. Not only are they familiar with the quotation, they like it. They don't argue with it or try to prove it isn't true. Most of them will say they want to live by it. However, most of them don't. The vast majority of Christians I know do not live lives that consistently *glorify God*, and they certainly don't appear to be *enjoying Him forever*.

Why not? If they know they should, and they want to, why don't they? You might be thinking, "Because they're just sinners, that's why!" And that's true – at least it's partially true. They are sinners; however, they are much more than *just* sinners. They are sinners who have been *transformed* by regeneration in Jesus Christ. What they *were*, they are no longer. Sin is no longer master over them because the Holy Spirit now dwells within them and enables them to obey God. *Every* Christian has the ability to glorify God and enjoy Him forever.

So why don't they? Two reasons come to mind: (1) They know very little of the truth contained in God's Word, and (2) They have never learned how to apply the scriptural truth they do know in everyday life.

Know what you are studying.

These studies were written to help women learn how to glorify and enjoy God by living out their transformation in Jesus Christ. They reflect the author's commitment to the Bible as the infallible, inerrant, authoritative and entirely sufficient Word of God to man, and her belief that Reformed theology is the clearest and most accurate statement of God's biblical revelation.

If you are new to Bible study or have doubts about the infallibility, inerrancy, authority or sufficiency of Scripture, you would benefit greatly from a study such as *A Book Like No Other: What's So Special About the Bible.*[2] You cannot effectively live out your transformation in Jesus Christ without understanding the nature and character of God's unique revelation in Scripture. If you are unfamiliar with Reformed Theology, begin your study by reading Appendix B, "What is Reformed Theology?"

If you have been studying the Bible for any length of time, you are probably aware of three basic kinds of studies. **Topical studies** present biblical principles regarding a particular *topic*, such as salvation, prayer, love, forgiveness, anger or worry, and encourage you to grow in your faith by stressing *practical application* of those principles. **Exegetical studies** focus on examining specific portions of Scripture (usually a book or a section of a book) verse by verse and concentrate on discovering the meaning of the passage under consideration. **Overview studies** step back and survey sweeping vistas, usually in summary form, with the intent of building a dependable framework for exegetical and topical studies.

All three types of studies should be included in a balanced "Bible study diet" that will be most nourishing for a growing Christian. The studies in the *Faith at Work* series are something of a combination; they examine specific passages of the book of James verse by verse, but they also concentrate on specific topics contained within those verses.

Know what to watch out for.

Exegetical and overview studies are extremely important and nourishing for growing Christians, but they sometimes stop short of *practical application*. Whenever you undertake an exegetical or overview study, be sure you follow through by applying what you have learned in your daily life.

Topical studies are very beneficial because they stimulate believers to grow and mature in their faith; however, they are prone to at least two pitfalls that require alertness on your part: (1) context abuse, and (2) selective proof texting.

Context abuse occurs when a verse or passage is isolated from its surroundings to support a point. For example, how many times have you heard Matthew 18:20 ("For where two or three have gathered together in My name, there I am in their midst.") or Matthew 18:19 ("Again I say to you, that if two of you agree on earth about anything that they may ask, it shall be done for them by my Father who is in heaven.") referenced in teaching about prayer? Actually, those verses were spoken by Jesus in a discussion of what is commonly known as church discipline, not prayer. Unfortunately, many erroneous doctrines about prayer have been built on this abuse of context.

Selective proof texting occurs when only those verses that seem to support a particular view are cited while those that could be used to refute that view are ignored. You may have heard *selective proof texting* in discussions about whether salvation can be lost or forfeited. Those who say a believer can lose his or her salvation may refer to Galatians 5:4, Hebrews 6:4-5, Hebrews 10:26-27, and 2 Peter 3:17 and neglect to mention John 10:27-30 or Romans 8:31-39, while those who hold the other view will do just the opposite. It's no wonder people say, "You can prove anything you want from the Bible."

Topical studies require you to follow the example of the noble Bereans in Acts 17 by "examining the Scriptures daily, to see whether these things [are] so." (v. 11) Even if you are new to Bible study, you can follow the example of these noble Bereans by developing the habit of (1) always checking the context of isolated verses, and (2) identifing what else the Bible says about the subject you are studying.

Check the context. The Bible was not originally written with chapter and verse designations. Those were added later by translators to make it easier for readers to find specific ideas. The Bible was originally written in sentences and paragraphs like any other piece of literature. Remembering this will help you check the context of isolated verses.

Locate the verse in question in your Bible and identify where the *sentence* in which it occurs begins and ends. (Some verses are complete sentences, but most are not.) Now determine where the paragraph containing that sentence begins and ends.[3] Read the entire paragraph to identify the subject being discussed, and ask yourself, what does the isolated verse say about this subject? If you have time, read the surrounding paragraphs to get an even broader idea of the verse's context. Then go back to the study material and ask yourself if the author used the verse appropriately in relation to its subject matter.

Identifying what else Scripture says on the subject. There are several ways you can do this. Begin by checking the cross-references in your Bible. These will direct you to other verses where the same words or ideas are discussed.

You may also want to invest in and learn how to use an *exhaustive concordance*. These invaluable reference books list every word in the Bible followed by a list of the verses where each word appears; and many of them also contain a numbering system allowing you to identify and define the original Hebrew and Greek words that were translated into English. These concordances are usually fairly expensive, so be sure to get the most for your money by buying the one that corresponds to the particular translation you use for study. If you need help learning how to use your concordance, ask your pastor, an elder, or other helpful, studious Christians.

A topical Bible like *Nave's* can also be very helpful because it lists references by topics, allowing you to access verses that may discuss the same idea in different words.

Of course, the best way to identify what else the Bible has to say on a particular subject is to become very familiar with the Bible as a whole. This is why a systematic reading program that structures daily readings to get you through the Bible in a definite time period is so important. Most of these take you "through the Bible in a year," but the time period is not all that important. What *is* important is that you are reading the entire Bible on a regular basis so you begin to become familiar with its overall message. Soon you will find yourself remembering (on your own!) where appropriate cross references are located. A good Scripture memorization program also helps with this process.

Know with whom you will study.

Ideally, you should pursue both individual study and group study of the Bible. Studying the Bible individually allows the Holy Spirit to deal with you on a very personal basis, while group study allows you to learn from other people's insights. If your time is limited, get involved with a group study, but prepare the material individually ahead of time. This way, one set of study materials can do double-duty.

Know how to prepare yourself for study.

Bible study is a serious task that requires careful preparation. It should never be undertaken in a haphazard manner. Take the time to prepare yourself physically, mentally, and spiritually so you can give your best effort to the Lord.

Physical preparation: Study when you are well-rested and alert. Establish a time and place that is quiet, free of distractions and conducive to concentration. Get in the habit of taking notes on what you read, and spend some time developing a filing system so you can find those notes later!

Mental preparation: Approach Bible study as you would any task that requires thoughtful effort to do well. Expect it to challenge you and stretch your thinking. Expect it to be difficult at times. And expect it to be extremely rewarding. Spend some time thinking about your daily routine and identify activities that should be limited or eliminated to give you the time you will need to pursue Bible study in a responsible manner. Then schedule blocks of time in your day for study. If you think you can study effectively "whenever the mood hits you," you should think again.

Spiritual preparation: Always begin your study time in prayer. Ask the Lord to reveal sin in your life that needs to be confessed and cleansed, to help you concentrate on His truths, and to illumine your mind to understand what He has written. End your study with a prayer for opportunities to apply what you have learned and wisdom to recognize those opportunities when they occur.

Know whose you are.

Never forget that Bible study equips you *to glorify God and enjoy Him forever.* You glorify God when you live in such a way that those around you look at you and see an accurate reflection of God's character and nature. You enjoy God when you are fully satisfied and content in His providential ordering of the circumstances of your life. When your life glorifies God and your joy is rooted in His providence, your impact on our fallen world will be tremendous.

I believe John MacArthur expressed these truths very well when he said, "An uncompromising life is characterized by an unashamed boldness that calls us to an uncommon standard. Allow God to do with your life as He pleases, that He might broaden your influence and glorify Himself."

Know how to approach the study questions.

Each lesson in this study is followed by three types of questions: **review questions, application questions** and

digging deeper questions. The *review questions* will help you determine how well you understood the lesson material by giving you an opportunity to express the key points of the lesson in your own words. The *application questions* encourage you to put your understanding of the lesson material to work in your daily life, and the *digging deeper questions* challenge you to pursue further study in certain key areas.

You should be able to find the answers to the *review questions* in the lesson material itself, but please resist the temptation to copy words or phrases out of the lesson when you answer these questions. Work at putting these ideas into your own words. When you can do this, you know you have understood what you have read. It might help to ask yourself, "How would I explain this idea to someone else if I didn't have the book with me?"

You should answer at least one of the *application questions*. If you do not have time to answer all of them, pray over them and ask the Lord to show you which one(s) *He* wants you to work on. Remember you are applying what you learned in the lesson material to your daily life, so these applications should take some time and thought— and they should be very specific. Avoid vague generalities.

An example illustrating the difference between vague generalities and specific applications might be helpful here. If you are applying the truths found in Philippians 2:3-4 about regarding others as more important than yourself by looking out for their interests, a vague generality would be: "I need to be more helpful and kind to those around me." A specific application would be: "I will call my daughter this morning (who lives in a sorority house on the local college campus) and cheerfully offer to type her term paper while she studies for her final exams. If she accepts my offer, I will do my Saturday chores on Friday instead, leaving Saturday free to help her." Do you see the difference? A specific application answers the questions:

Who?   My daughter

What?   Call and volunteer to type her paper; rearrange my chores

When?   Call this morning; type the paper Saturday; do the chores on Friday

Where?   Call from my living room; type the paper at home on my computer or in her room on her computer whichever is more convenient for her

How?   Cheerfully

A vague generality does not answer these questions. You can make applications in the areas of your thinking, your attitudes, and your behavior. Just remember to be specific! Vague generalities do not help you grow in your faith and do not glorify God. (See Lesson 6 of the Light for Your Path study, "Turning on the Light" for more information about application.[4])

Digging Deeper Questions usually require a significant amount of time and effort to complete. They were designed to provide a challenge for mature Christians who are eager for more advanced study. However, even if you are a new Christian who has done very little Bible study, read these questions and think about them. It will be good for you to be aware of some of these issues so you can be alert to material you may come across that relates to them.

Remember that you grow by stretching beyond where you are right now, so if one or two of these questions intrigue you, spend some time working on them. And, do not hesitate to ask for help from your pastor, elders or mature Christian friends.

As you work through this study, resist the temptation to compete with other Christians in your group. The purpose of this study is to help you grow in your faith by learning and applying God's truth in your daily life— not to fill up a study book with brilliantly worded answers. If you learn and apply *one element* of God's truth in each lesson, you are consistently moving beyond where you were when you began. Your goal is growth that glorifies God, not impressiveness that glorifies you. Don't ever forget that.

[1] "The Shorter Catechism with Scripture Proofs, Carlisle, PA: The Banner of Truth Trust, nd. p. 1.

[2] This study will be available from P&R Publishing Co. early in 1998. Any of the following resources will also help you resolve these issues in your mind:

> James M. Boice, *Standing on the Rock*. Grand Rapids: Baker Books, 1994.

> John MacArthur, Jr., *How to Get the Most from God's Word*. Dallas: Word Publishing, 1997.

> Josh McDowell, *Evidence That Demands a Verdict*. San Bernardino, CA: Here's Life Publishers, Inc., 1972, 1979.

> B. B. Warfield, *The Inspiration and Authority of the Bible*. Phillipsburg, NJ: Presbyterian and Reformed Publishing Co., 1948.

3 Some Bibles are formatted in paragraphs while others use bold type or a figure such as this ¶ to mark paragraphs. Check the introductory material in your Bible to determine how to identify paragraphs.

4 This study will be available from P&R Publishing Co. early in 1998.

James on Trials

James 1:2-25

How Faith Matures
in the Storms of Life

"A saving faith is a living and active faith;
it proves that it is alive by what it does.
The reality of a living faith is
demonstrated by its reaction under
adversity."

D. Edmond Hiebert

"When we allow the troubles of the world to interfere with living out a confident faith in God's absolute sovereignty over every circumstance of life, we rob Him of the glory He deserves and deny ourselves the contentment He wants us to experience in our relationship with Him."

Chapter One

Trouble, Trouble, Everywhere

Susan sighed heavily as she dropped the morning newspaper back on her desk and fought off the familiar temptation to cancel her subscription. After a week of discipling women who were struggling with everything from unfaithful husbands and rebellious children to terminal diseases and crippling car accidents, she instinctively recoiled from the graphic reminders of the "wages of sin" so carefully and objectively detailed on the pages of the Daily Journal. *"Oh Lord," she groaned, burying her face in her hands. "How do we deal with all this trouble..."*

All of us can identify with Susan. Every time we turn on the evening news, glance at the front page of our daily newspaper, or chat over coffee with friends, we are reminded of the Bible's affirmation that "Man is born for trouble, as sparks fly upward." (Job 5:7)

Trials, difficulties, and suffering are an inevitable part of life, and Christians aren't immune from any of them. Jesus said, "In the world you have tribulation." (John 16:33). Peter told his readers not to be surprised at the fiery ordeal among them (1 Peter 4:12). And Paul assured Timothy that he could expect persecution as a normal part of the Christian life (2 Timothy 3:12).

It is very easy to allow all the trouble in the world to permeate our thinking, shape our attitudes and control our behavior. Frightening images of potential disaster lurk in our minds as we grow increasingly apprehensive and frantically try to learn more effective ways to protect ourselves. Preventing, avoiding, or surviving an incalculable number of possible harms becomes our chief focus in life. Is this the way Jesus Christ wants His followers to live? Of course it isn't.

Jesus Christ does not want us to live this way for two very important reasons: (1) It doesn't glorify God, and (2) It doesn't benefit us. Glorifying God amounts to living in a way that accurately reflects His character and nature to those around us. When our lives glorify God, they constantly put His attributes on display for all to see.

When we allow the trouble in the world to consume us and control us, we do not glorify God because we conceal the most basic element of God's nature—His sovereignty—behind a wall of fear and unbelief. Our lives lie about God by depicting Him as One who really isn't powerful enough or caring enough to triumph over evil and work all things together for our good.

Several years ago, a popular book concluded that bad things happen to good people because even though God would really like to help us, He just can't. That picture of God is not only categorically false, it is absolutely terrifying. If God is not big enough and strong enough to control evil within the boundaries He sets for it, why should we have any confidence in Him at all? Is He even God? By definition, no, He is not.

Fixing our attention on the trouble in the world also fails to benefit us. It denies God's promises that His plans for us are for our welfare to give us a future and a hope (Jeremiah 29:11), and that He will not allow anything unbearable to come into our lives (1 Corinthians 10:13). It clogs the channels of free-flowing joy and hinders the performance of life-fulfilling service.

When we allow the troubles of the world to interfere with living out a confident faith in God's absolute sovereignty over every circumstance in life, we rob Him of the glory He deserves and deny ourselves the contentment He wants us to experience in our relationship with Him.

The way we respond to trials tells us a great deal about our faith. All genuine believers in Jesus Christ have abundant resources *in their faith* to face and overcome any trial they may encounter in this life (2 Corinthians 9:8; Philippians 4:19; 2 Peter 1:3-4). Unfortunately, merely possessing such resources does not guarantee that believers will use them effectively when faced with life's difficulties.

Several years ago, I was flying home from a wedding in Los Angeles when one of the airplane's engines blew out. A sudden, terrifying, metallic *twaang* brought the beverage service to an abrupt halt, while several passengers on the right side of the aircraft actually ducked as oil sprayed across their windows. I immediately panicked and thoroughly embarrassed my fifteen-year- old daughter who was sitting next to me. (Fifteen-year olds are easily embarrassed by their parents, but in this case her embarrassment was legitimate!) Since then I have gone to great lengths to avoid flying in airplanes.

Only recently have I come to grips with the full import of my behavior. My panic in the midst of a frightening situation may have been "understandable," but it certainly didn't honor the God I serve nor did it validate what I had been teaching about Him for years.

By allowing fear to overrule everything I knew to be true about God, I failed to glorify Him and missed a golden opportunity to minister to those around me who were frightened with very good reason because they were not prepared to die. I also failed to be an example of living faith that my daugher could follow.

My avoidance of airplanes has done nothing but compound the problem. It tells those around me that my fear of flying is greater than my faith in God. I have tried to tell myself that there is nothing wrong with preferring one means of travel over another, but in my heart, I know my refusal to fly has very little to do with preference. Rather, it has a great deal to do with the extent of my willingness to live in accordance with what I say I believe.

My response to this trial has taught me a lot about faith. It's taught me that it's easier to talk about faith than it is to live it, and that it's easier to teach about faith in a classroom than it is to learn about it from personal experience. It has also taught me that I would rather be safe than honor God. Basically, it has taught me a great deal about the degree of my own depravity and the magnitude of God's grace.

Even though I have consistently failed to glorify Him in this area of my life for several years, He has patiently dealt with me until I am now ready to repent, confess this sin and turn from it. Today I purchased an airline ticket, and in a little less than two months I will use it to visit my mother.

Facing my fear of flying may seem like a relatively insignificant "trial" in a world filled with horrible misery and suffering, but its significance increases exponentially when you understand that it came as a definitive answer to one of my own prayers. As I have grown in my faith, I have repeatedly asked God to prepare me for useful service in His Kingdom. I now understand that part of that preparation is learning to trust Him in all situations—no matter how uncomfortable, discouraging or frightening they may be.

Trusting God involves learning the truth about who He is and how He operates as well as putting that knowledge into practice in daily life. If I want to be entrusted with great things, I must learn to trust Him in the small things. For me, getting on an airplane is a small thing that has become a major obstacle to my continued growth as an effective Christian. That obstacle must be cleared before I can move on.

When God blessed me with saving faith in Jesus Christ, He equipped me to handle *any* situation of life in a way that would glorify Him while benefiting me. *However,* simply possessing that ability did not guarantee results. In order to become proficient at living by faith, I have to practice what I know. The more I practice, the more natural it becomes.

Responding to difficult circumstances in a manner that glorifies God is part of what the Bible calls *maturity in Christ.* God wants His children to become mature because their maturity glorifies Him as it benefits them; therefore, He is faithful to give us opportunities to mature by practicing our faith. Most of these opportunities come in the form of trials, difficulties, and suffering.

Since we humans have a built-in aversion to suffering, we frequently wonder why our all-powerful and all-knowing God couldn't have come up with some other way to help us grow. Volumes have been written in an attempt to explain *why* a good God allows His people to suffer, and many of them make for fascinating reading, especially for those with a philosophical mind set. But when all the words have been said, read, written and digested, the basic answer is always the same: A faithful Christian's response to suffering is something the world cannot duplicate and for which it has no legitimate substitute. As such, it is a tremendous testimony of both the existence and perfection of God. When professing Christians fail to respond faithfully to suffering, their lives tell lies about God.

So, the way we face trials tells us something very important about our faith—how mature it really is. A Christian with immature faith will avoid trials and seek to escape them at all costs, while a more mature Christian will tend to see them as opportunities to trust God as the means of his own growth and God's glory.

Responding to trials with mature faith doesn't happen automatically, nor does it occur overnight. It's an acquired response that becomes habitual only as we study God's Word and take advantage of the opportunities God gives us to practice what we have learned in the power of the Holy Spirit.

The first chapter of the book of James[1] describes this process in a very clear and forthright manner.

- Verses 2-12 describe a proper *attitude* toward trials.

- Verses 13-18 describe how a trial degenerates into a *temptation* to sin.

- Verses 19-25 describe ungodly and godly *responses* to trials.

---

1 James has been accused of teaching salvation by works; however, a careful reading of the second chapter of this book reveals no differences between the Apostle Paul and James in the area of saving faith. What appears to be differences in their writings result from their equally intense efforts to support the concept of salvation by grace through faith to two entirely different groups of detractors.

A great deal of Paul's teaching was directed toward people who wanted to add their own works to God's grace, while James found himself squaring off against those who wanted to use God's grace as justification for antinomianism (the idea that behavior is unrelated to faith, or that Christians are not bound by moral law). When we study the teachings of Paul and James as two sides of the same coin—the coin of saving faith—we come away with a better understanding of the coin. Saving faith is wholly *by* grace, but it is also a faith that *works*.

Review Questions

1. What does the Bible teach about trials, difficulties, and suffering in the Christian life? (Include Scripture references.)

2. Explain what it means "to glorify God."

3. How does the way a Christian responds to trials determine how effectively he or she will glorify God?

4. What does the way a Christian responds to trials indicate about his or her faith?

5. Why does God want us to become mature in our faith?

6. Why does God permit (or require) us to suffer?

Applying the Word

1. Describe a trial you have faced at some point in your
    Christian life.

2. How did you respond to this trial?

3. Did your response glorify God? How or how not?

4. Did your response benefit you spiritually? Explain.

5. Do you need to repent, confess, and turn from any sin associated with your response to this trial? If so, confide in a mature Christian friend or relative who will encourage you and hold you accountable to follow through with the action you need to take.

Digging Deeper

1. Read and study 2 Corinthians 11:16-12:10. What kind of
    difficulties, trials, and suffering did Paul endure during his
    life? How did he respond to them? Did his response glorify
    God? Explain. Did his response benefit him? Explain.

2. Have you had to endure difficulties and trials like those Paul went through? How can his example encourage you in your struggles?

*"James is not appealing to our emotions here but to our minds. He is not telling us how we should **feel** about trials, but what we should **think** about them."*

Chapter Two

What are You so Happy About?

Consider it all joy, my brethren, when you encounter various trials, knowing that the testing of your faith produces endurance. And let endurance have its perfect result, that you may be perfect and complete, lacking in nothing. (James 1:2-4)

A friend of mine is fond of saying, "Keep smiling. It makes people wonder what you've been up to." The slightly humorous cynicism lurking behind that statement is, unfortunately, all too characteristic of our society these days. We wonder about people who are happy all the time. We figure they *must* be up to something or completely out of touch with reality.

When we look at the world around us, we don't see a lot to be happy about. Perhaps that's why the opening words of the book of James are so shocking to the modern reader, but probably no more so than they were to his original audience. Contrary to what some may think, the world hasn't changed all that much in two thousand years.

First century Christians didn't have a great deal to be happy about either. The difficulties faced by first and twentieth century Christians (and all those in between) may be vastly different in content, but they are very similar in effect. Life in a fallen world has always made the "pursuit of happiness" a very elusive venture.

A careful reading of James's opening words in verse 2 indicates that he is not being at all sarcastic or cynical when he says, "*Consider it all joy...*when you encounter various trials."

The word *consider* has to do with a mental attitude adopted after due deliberation. James is not appealing to our emotions here but to our minds. He is not telling us how we should *feel* about trials, but what we should *think* about them.

The words "feel" and "think" are used synonymously by most people today, which is indeed unfortunate because the two words do not mean the same thing. "Feeling" is an emotional process, while "thinking" is a mental one. If you are home alone on a dark, stormy night and hear someone breaking in through the back door, you will *feel* fear—but you will *think* about calling 911.

This distinction is important because mental processes are behaviors subject to willful control whereas feelings are not. If I wait for my *feelings* to change, chances are I will never get on that airplane to visit my mother. It's going to take my willful mental determination to obey the Lord, in spite of my feelings, to get me off the ground!

Christians should concern themselves with what they can control—their thinking—knowing that godly thinking develops godly attitudes which will, in turn, affect their emotional responses.

An attitude is a general mental perspective that colors the way we look at life. Optimism, pessimism, humility, and arrogance can all be regarded as attitudes that develop as a result of habitual patterns of thinking. The joy James refers to in verse 2 can be described as an attitude that develops in response to habitually thinking about trials with a godly perspective.

This attitude of joy bears very little resemblance to what the world calls happiness. The Christian's attitude of joy is rooted in the peace that results from knowing we are in the sovereign care of the all-powerful God of the Universe who works all things together for our good (Romans 8:28; Hebrews 13:5).

What the world calls happiness on the other hand, is inexorably tied to people, circumstances and possessions. Worldly happiness slips from my grasp when people act up, circumstances go awry, and possessions disappear, but an attitude of joy endures through all of these things because God never changes.

We can *consider* our trials *all joy* by focusing our minds on what James tells us about them. They are an indispensable part of our growth as Christians. Trials require us to exercise our faith, producing within us the quality of endurance. Endurance eventually brings us to the point of being "perfect and complete, lacking in nothing," a beautiful description of maturity in Christ. When we discipline our minds to focus on the beneficial results of trials, we can learn to face them with an attitude of joy even when we don't feel happy about our circumstances.

Since attitudes grow out of godly thought patterns, a Christian's attitudes should be firmly grounded in Scripture. God designed our minds to lead and control our emotions (Proverbs 22:17-18; Isaiah 26:3; Romans 8:6-7; 12:1-2; 2 Corinthians 11:3; Philippians 2:2; 4:8-9; Colossians 3:2; 1 Peter 1:13). When we allow our emotions to overrule our minds in responding to a trial, we will inevitably miss God's intended purpose for the trial. Without trials, our faith would remain weak and untested, and we would not develop the maturity necessary for effective service in God's kingdom.

Strengthening our faith by exercising it in response to trials is an essential part of the process Scripture calls *sanctification*. Our salvation in Jesus Christ includes three primary aspects: justification, sanctification, and glorification. Justification is a legal transaction whereby God declares us righteous on the basis of Christ's atoning sacrifice on the cross. This imputed righteousness allows us to stand in God's presence on the merits of Christ rather than our own.

Glorification occurs when we are translated from this fallen world to the perfect world of heaven. The pollution of sin will be removed from us permanently and our actual righteousness will equal our imputed righteousness.

Sanctification is what happens in between. Obviously God does not save us and take us immediately to heaven. He leaves us here in a fallen world to reflect His glory as we do the work He prepared for us before the world began. Responding to trials in faithful dependence on Him is part of that work, and displays His character dramatically.

When one of my friends was going through a severe trial, she kept saying to me, "This trial would be so much easier to endure if I only knew the reason behind it." Finally, more out of frustration than wisdom, I asked her, "What if the only reason for this trial is to give you a platform on which to display God's sufficiency to enable you to endure it?"

The Greek word for endurance (*hupomeno*) means "to remain under," and is used almost exclusively to refer to enduring difficult circumstances. Endurance is an integral part of the sanctification process because it draws us close to God by strengthening our dependence on Him, sharpening our ability to serve Him, and magnifying our love for Him.

My friend has learned that endurance produces great blessings that may not include elimination of the trial. Her life has become a constant testimony to God's sufficiency in any situation and an encouragement to others who are facing difficulty. I can't help but wonder if those who have endured the most on earth will find the joys of heaven all the more intense because of it.

You may be thinking, "Good for her; she must be some kind of super-saint. The trial I am going through has soured my outlook on life, and I'm not sure I'll ever have a godly attitude toward it. So, what should I do?" You'll be interested to know that her attitude wasn't right at first either, and didn't change until she committed herself to seeking God's wisdom in prayer. That is the subject of Chapter 3.

Review Questions

1. In your own words, distinguish between the words "feel" and "think." Why is this distinction important?

2. What is an attitude? Is it more related to thinking or feeling? Explain why James's words "Consider it all joy" describe an attitude rather than a feeling.

3. Explain the difference between the attitude of joy described in the Bible and what the world calls happiness.

4. Define *endurance*. Why is endurance important in the Christian life? Describe some of the blessings of endurance.

5. List and describe the three primary aspects of salvation. How is endurance related to one of these? Optional: Is it related to the other two? Why or why not?

Applying the Word

1. What kinds of things make you happy? List as many of these
    as you can on a piece of paper. On another piece of paper,
    make two columns, one entitled "Worldly Happiness" and
    the other entitled "Biblical Attitude of Joy." Place each item
    on your list in one of these two columns. Which list is
    longer? How would your thinking have to change in order
    to move some of the items from the "Worldly Happiness"
    column to the "Biblical Attitude of Joy" column?

2. Describe a trial you have experienced since you became a Christian. Did you learn endurance from this trial? Why or why not? If you did learn endurance, how did this help you mature in Christ? What specific blessings did you receive from your endurance?

Digging Deeper

1. Read and study Philippians 4:4-13. Explain why Paul has no problem commanding the Philippians to be joyful. If he considered joy primarily an emotion, do you think he would command them to rejoice? Why or why not? How does Paul connect joy with peace? How does he relate thinking and behavior to joy? Finally, how does joy relate to contentment?

2. Explain how the man who endured all the suffering described in 2 Corinthians 11:23-29 could have the attitude of joy described in Philippians 4:4-13.

"... the greatest challenge involved in facing a trial is disciplining our minds to seek wisdom from God when we would rather give in to our emotions."

Chapter Three

Asking the Right Questions

But if any of you lacks wisdom, let him ask of God, who gives to all men generously and without reproach, and it will be given to him. But let him ask in faith without any doubting, for the one who doubts is like the surf of the sea driven and tossed by the wind. For let not that man expect that he will receive anything from the Lord, being a double-minded man, unstable in all his ways. (James 1:5-8)

Experiencing a trial is never pleasant. Even when we understand that God uses trials to perfect us for His service, we don't eagerly anticipate their arrival. If you are anything like me, you keep hoping God will come up with some other way to help you grow!

Because trials are, by definition, *unpleasant* experiences, they tend to generate *emotional* responses. Trials are trials because they make us feel miserable. That is why the greatest challenge involved in facing a trial is disciplining our minds to seek wisdom from God when we would rather give in to our emotions. At times like these, we are frequently tempted to close our Bibles, stay home from church, and avoid prayer while we lick our wounds, vent our anger toward God and wallow in self-pity. If we do turn to God, we tend to seek from Him all the wrong things.

When my father died several years ago, my mother went through a very emotional time. She was recovering from major cancer surgery when my father was hospitalized with suspected phlebitis. Three weeks later, just a few days shy of their forty-eighth wedding anniversary, he died. As if that wasn't enough, she and my father had been struggling at this time with some difficult relational issues with both my sister and me. Like I said, it was a very emotional time.

Shock got her through the funeral, and then the emotional bomb went off. She told me later the hardest part was trying to deal with so many emotions at once. Anger, grief, loneliness, frustration, and fear always seemed to attack in waves, leaving in their wake a huge temptation to sink into self-pity. Fortunately, my mother learned to seek *God's wisdom* for her trial, and responded well to the Lord's blessing on her first feeble efforts to honor Him in the midst of calamity. She learned, as Paul did so many centuries ago, that when we are weak, He is strong.

James tells us, in verses 5-8 of chapter 1, that *considering it all joy when we encounter trials* involves *seeking wisdom in faith* from the Lord and avoiding the perils of *instability and double-mindedness*. When we are drowning in the emotional onslaught of a trial, James tells us to go to God in prayer seeking *wisdom* to deal with the trial—not escape from the trial, not additional resources to deal with the trial, not even a fuller understanding of the trial. God commended Solomon for seeking wisdom when he could have asked for anything (1 Kings 3:5-14; 4:29-30), and He wants us to do the same (Proverbs 23:23; Ephesians 1:17; Colossians 1:9).

Scripture equates wisdom with discernment, understanding, righteousness, and the fear of the Lord (Proverbs 9:10; 10:13,23,31). Therefore, when we seek wisdom to deal with a trial, we are seeking to understand and respond to the trial with a godly perspective. We are asking God to help us see the trial as He sees it and to respond to it in a way that accomplishes His purposes for it. We can take such a self-sacrificing request to God without fear, knowing that He is our generous, loving Father who will not give us more than we can bear (1 Corinthians 10:13) and who sovereignly works all things together for our good (Romans 8:28-29).

My mother felt overwhelmed by the prospects of widowhood. She had never lived alone, and had always depended on my father to take care things like mowing the lawn, fixing the furnace, and paying the taxes.

He was a true "southern gentleman" who believed women should be protected from the harsh realities of life as they were encouraged to develop their unique womanly virtues. Nearly half a century with this man had left my mother extremely capable in some areas and totally unskilled in others. Facing perhaps a decade or more of life without her "other half" was pretty unnerving.

As she struggled with her trial, she began to see that she was looking at the situation from *her* perspective. She was evaluating her circumstances in light of *her* abilities, *her* shortcomings, *her* fears, and *her* desires. She had a distorted view of the trial because she was looking at it in the light of her own earthly wisdom rather than the pure light of "the wisdom from above." (James 3:17)

Before she could begin to deal with the trial in a manner that would honor God and benefit her, she needed to seek *His will* for her in the situation. As she did that, she needed to avoid the doubt that would lead to double-mindedness and instability.

James reminds us that we have the privilege of praying in faith without doubt. That privilege rests on our standing in Jesus Christ and our confidence in God's revealed attributes. Our standing in Christ guarantees our access to God (John 14:6; Acts 4:12), and our confidence in His attributes assures us that He always does what is right (Psalm 145:17; Hosea 14:9; 1 Peter 2:23).

Doubt reveals one of two things: a lack of assurance regarding our salvation, or a failure to believe that God will do what is right. Doubt prevents us from implementing the very wisdom we need to deal with the trial in a manner that honors God and benefits us. Therefore, before we seek God's wisdom to handle the trial, we must settle our doubts by examining ourselves to see if we are in the faith (2 Corinthians 13:5), and reminding ourselves of the nature and character of our great God. (The book of Isaiah is a good place to start.)

James refers to a man who doubts as double-minded and unstable. James may have coined the term "double-minded," as no other New Testament author uses it, and it is not found in pagan authors before the time of James.[1] It's a very expressive word in the Greek, meaning "a man two-souled." Such a man lives as if he possessed two separate personalities, one that knows and believes God and one that doesn't. He is characteristically unstable in all his ways because he has no solid foundation upon which to stand. God has no use for him and will not give him wisdom he would be incapable of appropriating.

The fact that we are instructed to seek wisdom, in faith without doubting, does not endorse the popular practice of "taking authority" over a trial by attempting to banish a responsible demon or demand a personally satisfying outcome. Biblical wisdom submits to God's sovereign control over the nature, duration, and outcome of a trial while recognizing that God alone is capable of seeing the circumstances of life from an eternal perspective. We are simply too short-sighted to demand the right to control the course of life's trials.

The faith James is talking about here is saving faith grounded in God's work through Jesus Christ, not faith in our ability to believe in the efficacy of our own words; and the doubting he refers to is doubting God, not doubting ourselves.

[1] D. Edmond Hiebert, *James*. (Chicago: Moody Press, 1992), 74.

Review Questions

1. What is the greatest challenge in facing a trial? Why is this challenge so great?

2. Explain the connection between seeking God's wisdom in the midst of a trial and considering the trial an occasion for joy.

3. How does doubt interfere with seeking wisdom to face a trial?

4. What do John 14:6 and Acts 4:12 teach us about our privilege of coming to God in prayer? (You may have to think about this a bit.)

5. Explain the term "double-minded." Why would a double-minded man be unstable in all his ways?

Applying the Word

1. Describe your response to a trial you faced early in your Christian walk. Did your mind or your emotions control your response? Did your response honor God by seeking His wisdom for the trial? If not, what could you have done differently to take advantage of the trial as an opportunity to glorify God and mature in your faith?

2. Do you know someone who is going through a trial right now? If so, how can you help them understand what you have learned so far in this study? Be as specific as you can.

Digging Deeper

1. Read carefully Isaiah 40-55, and record everything you find about God's character and nature. How does this "character sketch of God" impact your attitude toward trials?

"All people, rich or poor alike, must look to the Lord as their sufficiency during times of trial because salvation has a wonderful way of leveling worldly distinctions."

Chapter Four

Rich Man, Poor Man

But let the brother of humble circumstances glory in his high position; and let the rich man glory in his humiliation, because like flowering grass he will pass away. For the sun rises with a scorching wind, and withers the grass; and its flower falls off, and the beauty of its appearance is destroyed; so too the rich man in the midst of his pursuits will fade away. (James 1:9-11)

One of the most intriguing stories in the New Testament concerns a *brother of humble circumstances* and a *rich man*. Onesimus was a humble slave who was owned by Philemon, a rich man who lived in Colossae. Philemon had been led to faith in Jesus Christ by the Apostle Paul and eventually established a church in his spacious Colossian home.

His slave Onesimus, for reasons about which we can only speculate, ran away from Philemon's household, and went to Rome, probably thinking it would be a good place to "disappear." In God's providence, he encountered the Apostle Paul, who was serving a prison sentence there, and soon became a Christian himself.

Within a short time, Onesimus had endeared himself to Paul by becoming useful to him in the ministry and a comfort to him in his imprisonment. However, Paul knew Onesimus could not stay in Rome. He had to return to Colossae to seek forgiveness from the master he had wronged.

Paul did everything he could to help Onesimus do the right thing. He wrote Philemon a personal letter, exerting all the power of his considerable influence to persuade his old friend to receive Onesimus as a brother instead of as a criminal. He also arranged for Onesimus to travel with Tychicus who had been given the responsibility of delivering Paul's letter to the Colossian believers who met in Philemon's home. By doing these things, he guaranteed a certain measure of safety for Onesimus and expressed his own confidence in the willingness of Onesimus to put his newfound faith into practice. Most of us recognize the story of Onesimus and Philemon as a striking example of the power of forgiveness within the Christian community, but we should also see it as an apt illustration of the truths taught in James 1:9-11.

All people, rich or poor alike, must look to the Lord as their sufficiency during times of trial because salvation has a wonderful way of leveling worldly distinctions. Galatians 3:28 tells us "There is neither Jew nor Greek, there is neither slave nor free man, there is neither male nor female; for you are all one in Christ Jesus," and Colossians 3:11 says, "A renewal in which there is no distinction between Greek and Jew, circumcised and uncircumcised, barbarian, Scythian, slave and freeman, but Christ is all, and in all."

We live in a prestige-conscious culture that exalts certain human characteristics and conditions and degrades others. The rich, powerful, intelligent, well-educated, beautiful and famous are elevated above the poor, weak, slow, poorly educated, ugly and unknown. Status-seeking, worldly humans beings take pride in the things that distinguish them from others and, at least in their own minds, make them a little better than their neighbors.

When a person is transformed through saving faith in Jesus Christ, all that changes. Salvation shifts our focus from self to Christ; therefore, the differences between Christians dissolve in the surpassing value of His glory. We become one in Christ because He is all and in all. Not only does this change the way we relate to one another, it also changes the way we handle trials.

James points out that the nature of the challenges inherent in all trials differ markedly depending on the circumstances of the individual facing the trial. The poor man may be tempted to blame his humble circumstances for the trial or to believe that he cannot deal with the trial effectively because of his lack of resources; while the rich man may be tempted to believe that trials are somehow beneath his dignity and to rely on his riches or influential position to escape the trial. Yielding to either temptation is sin.

It would have been natural for Onesimus to blame all his difficulties in life on his low social standing and to think that he could never overcome those difficulties as long as he remained a slave in Philemon's household. It would have been equally natural for Philemon to see a difficulty such as a runaway slave as an affront to his dignity and to use all the privileges of his high social standing and wealth to deal with the situation.

Both men would have been sinning if they had allowed their worldly circumstances to dictate their response to the trial. A poor man, like Onesimus, must remember that as a believer in Jesus Christ he has been united and exalted with Christ. His low position in this world does not hinder his being seated in the heavenlies with Christ Jesus (Ephesians 1). His union with the Lord provides him with unlimited spiritual resources to face and overcome trials in a way that furthers his own maturity in Christ and glorifies God (Philippians 4:19). None of God's children are disadvantaged.

The poor man's difficulties are not the result of his humble circumstances; they are the result of God's sovereign design. The poor man is not ill-equipped to overcome the trial; he has access to His Father's heavenly provision. God has promised Him everything—in abundance—to do the work he has been called to do (2 Corinthians 9:8). If he finds himself short of resources, he can be assured he is either under God's discipline for sin in his life, or he is trying to do work that God has not called him to do (Hebrews 12:5-11; James 4:13-16).

A rich man, like Philemon, must remember that he came to Christ in humility. Nothing concerning his worldly situation encouraged, enticed, or compelled God to save him; his salvation came entirely through God's gracious, effectual call. Just as his worldly position and wealth could not save him, neither does it exempt him from trials. The rich Christian must face and overcome difficulties in life for the same reason the poor Christian does—to grow in maturity and to glorify God. Worldly riches provide no advantage; the only truly beneficial resources are those stored up in heaven (Matthew 6:19-21).

Worldly wealth is not evil in itself. Many of God's faithful saints down through the ages have been rich in the world's goods. God is not nearly as concerned about the bottom line of our personal balance sheets as he is about our attitude toward Him.

Do we recognize that all we have, whether a little or a lot, comes from Him, and that it has been entrusted to us to use for His purposes, not our own? Do our daily lives reflect contentment, regardless of our circumstances? Are we willing to move between want and plenty, hardship and comfort at God's call without complaint? Are we willing to give up (or accept) any possession, privilege, or position to further God's kingdom? Are we willing to minister to anyone who has a need, and to receive ministry from anyone when we have a need? In other words, have we submitted our worldly situation completely to His control?

James understands that this kind of surrender is more difficult for a rich man like Philemon than it is for a poor man like Onesimus. The humility (indeed, the humiliation!) required to submit to God in salvation is far easier for one who has already learned humility from his worldly condition.

James's comments in verses 10-11 are reminiscent of his Savior's earlier statements to His disciples: "It is easier for a camel to go through the eye of a needle, than for a rich man to enter the kingdom of God." (Matthew 19:24). But we must not forget that Jesus also reminded them, "With men this is impossible, but with God all things are possible." (v. 26). Rich men can be saved and used mightily by God to accomplish His purposes, but in order to do so, they must remember that they are as transient as flowering grass and will one day fade away in the midst of their pursuits.

The poor brother and the rich brother must join hands in a common bond of submission to Christ, and face trials with the common goal of glorifying God by growing toward spiritual maturity, knowing that their perseverance will grant them the same prize—"the crown of life which the Lord has promised to those who love Him."

Review Questions

1. How might an individual's economic circumstances or social status affect the way he or she faces a trial?

2. Relate the story of Philemon and Onesimus to Galatians 3:28 and Colossians 3:11.

3. What does a poor man like Onesimus need to remember when he is facing a trial?

4. What does a rich man like Philemon need to remember when he is facing a trial?

5. Why does it seem more difficult for the rich to come to salvation than for the poor to do so?

Applying the Word

1. Read Philippians 4:10-19 and evaluate your contentment
    level in the light of Paul's words. Can you honestly say that
    you are content in every circumstance of life? Write down
    specific examples of discontentment in your life. What does
    your discontentment tell you about your view of God's
    sovereignty over the circumstances of your life?

2. Do you consider yourself rich or poor? Describe a time when your financial situation affected the way you responded to a trial. Did your response to the trial glorify God? If so, how? Did your response encourage you to exercise your faith in Christ? If so, how? If you were facing this same trial today, would you do anything differently? If so, what?

Digging Deeper

1. Study James 2:1-13 and 4:1-5,11. Use a concordance to look up and study other passages about wealth and answer the following questions.

   a. Is it sinful to be rich? Explain.

   b. Is financial wealth a sign of God's favor? Explain.

   c. What particular temptations to sin do the rich face that the poor do not?

   d. What opportunities for service do the rich enjoy that the poor do not?

e. Do you believe it is easier for a rich man or a poor man to live a life that honors God? Explain.

f. If you are not already, would you like to be rich? Why or why not?

"Perseverance through trials verifies the existence of God's love residing in us; thus, perseverance is the mark of a true saint..."

Chapter Five

The Crown of Life

Blessed is a man who perseveres under trial; for once he has been approved, he will receive the crown of life, which the Lord has promised to those who love Him. (James 1:12)

The story is told of a small southern town located in the heart of the Bible Belt that was home to two lively churches—one of the Baptist and one of the Methodist persuasion. These two churches had built impressive new buildings right next door to each other on the main street of town and seemed to thrive on friendly (and sometimes not so friendly) competition.

One Sunday morning in mid-June when all the windows in the new buildings were open wide for the enjoyment of the scrubbed and shiny congregations, the Baptist song leader rose to his feet and led his people in a stirring rendition of a popular old hymn, "Will there Be any Stars in My Crown?". Confident that the powerful singing of his congregation had "one-upped" the Methodist song leader next door, he sat down with a satisfied smile that quickly faded.

The Methodists had apparently been so impressed with the Baptists' musical query that they were moved to respond. Through the two sets of open windows the Baptist congregation could clearly hear the Methodists belting out the equally popular old hymn, "No, Not One!"

I have always found that story amusing—not only because it points out the silliness of much of the competition that goes on among Christians, but also because it illustrates the lack of biblical content in many of our popular hymns.

The Bible doesn't teach that our rewards in heaven will consist of a number of stars in a crown. Instead, it describes a number of different crowns that will be received by believers who have performed different types of service for God. One of those crowns is described here in James 1:12. Those who persevere under trials can look forward to receiving the *crown of life* which the Lord has promised to those who love Him.

Perseverance under trial is a measure of our love for the Lord—not the world's emotion-laden love, but the self-sacrificial *agape* described in 1 Corinthians 13:4-8a. We can love God in this way only when we have been so loved by Him first (1 John 4:19). *Agape* is not natural to human beings; its only source is God. Men and women who belong to God are always conduits of *agape,* never its source. God gives us His *agape* and then demands that we give it back to Him by denying ourselves, taking up our crosses (upon which we have crucified self) daily and following Him (Luke 9:23) anywhere He chooses to lead us.

When He leads through difficulties, and fear causes us to stumble, we must take refuge in the strength of His love for us. This is the very love He asks us to return to Him by trusting His provision and care in all circumstances. Perseverance through trials verifies the existence of God's love residing in us; thus, perseverance is the mark of a true saint, one who will be glorified with Christ.

The words "has been approved" in verse 12 carry the idea of testing for genuineness. We are *approved* by trials just as precious metals are tested by fire. In the refining process tons of ore go into the fire but only the genuine metal survives intact and purified. Likewise, Christians who go through God's refining process burn off ungodliness and worldliness until they stand before Him perfected and completed.

James 1:12 does not promise us that Christians will go through trials without trauma, pain, resistance, agony, distress, or discouragement. Christ's disciples are never promised immunity from the physical or emotional effects of trials, but when they seek God's wisdom (v. 5), they can endure these temporary effects with joy, because they understand the eternal value of the end result—their perfection and completion in Christ.

Those who are approved will receive the crown of life. Because this crown has been reserved for those who love the Lord, I am convinced that all believers will receive this crown. You simply cannot be a Christian without loving the Lord, and you can't love Him without following Him (Matthew 22:37-40; Titus 2:11-14). Not all Christians love and follow with the same consistency or intensity, but they all love and follow.

Being motivated to service in this life by the promise of rewards in heaven should be a manifestation of our love for Christ, not a selfish pursuit. If you have children, I'm sure you have struggled with this issue the same way I have from time to time. Is it right to reward your children (with money, special treats, favorite activities or whatever) for doing chores around the house, getting good grades, and behaving properly? Or by doing that, are you instilling a "what's-in-it-for-me" attitude that works against the qualities of responsibility and unselfishness you want to instill in them? Well, my only child is grown now and I'm still not sure I know the right answers to those questions; however, her response to receiving rewards for service and behavior helped me understand the principle behind the biblical concept of rewards in heaven for faithful believers.

When she was young, we did reward her financially for doing certain chores around the house and for getting good grades in school. By the age of twelve she had become a fairly efficient money manager. As a matter of fact, she had only one major weakness—buying gifts for her family and friends. She would work hard, save her money, and then thoroughly enjoy spending it *all* on other people. I began to wonder if I should try to correct this trait when I suddenly realized she was demonstrating in her life precisely what the Bible teaches about our rewards in heaven!

The book of Revelation contains one vivid description after another of the central activity of heaven, which will be worshipping God and Christ Jesus. Our focus will not be on our own accomplishments in Heaven; it will be on the glory of our Father and our Lord. We will not be parading around heaven, balancing our crowns on our egocentric heads and comparing ourselves to others. We will be using those rewards to honor God and Jesus Christ.

We *should* look forward to receiving rewards in heaven so we will have something to cast at the feet of our Lord. The properly motivated Christian "works for rewards in heaven" in anticipation of the sheer joy of having an abundance to give away in extravagant worship of the Lord to whom we owe everything worthwhile in life. Thus, piling up crowns in heaven becomes not a selfish motivation at all, but the purest and highest motivation of all.

Review Questions

1. Who will receive the crown of life and for what reason will they receive it?

2. Read 1 Corinthians 13:4-8a and describe the self-sacrificial *agape* love defined there.

3. What do 1 John 4:19 and Luke 9:23 tell us about self-sacrificial *agape* love?

4. Explain what James means when he says that those who persevere under trials will be *approved*.

5. Is looking forward to receiving crowns (rewards) in heaven a selfish desire? Why or why not?

Applying the Word

1. The following chart contains each characteristic of agape love listed in 1 Corinthians 13:4-8a. In the middle column of this chart list an example of how God's love toward you reflects each of these characteristics. In the right column list an example of how your love toward God and/or other people could display each of these characteristics. Be as specific as you can in your examples. Avoid generalities.

1 Corinthians 13:4-8a	God's Love	My Love
patient		
kind		
not jealous (does not envy)		
does not brag		
is not arrogant		
does not act unbecoming		
does not seek its own (is not self-seeking)		

1 Corinthians 13:4-8a	God's Love	My Love
is not provoked (is not easily angered)		
does not take into account a wrong suffered		
does not rejoice in unrighteousness		
rejoices in truth		
bears all things		
believes all things		
hopes all things		
endures all things		
never fails		

2. Based on the preceding chart, explain any connections you
    see between the way God first loved you and the way you
    should love God and others. Which specific characteristics of
    love are difficult for you? Which are easy? How can you
    begin to improve in those areas that are difficult for you?

Digging Deeper

1. Using a concordance and any other reliable biblical reference books, do a study on "crowns," and then fill in the following chart:

Name of crown	Who receives this crown	Reason for receiving this crown

Which crowns do you believe you will receive? Why?

*"A **peirasmos** can be either an opportunity to glorify God by relying on His strength to endure a trying situation and grow toward maturity; or it can be a temptation to sin by allowing ourselves to be enticed and carried away by our own lust."*

Chapter Six

This is a Test...This is Only a Test

Let no one say when he is tempted, "I am being tempted by God"; for God cannot be tempted by evil, and He Himself does not tempt anyone. But each one is tempted when he is carried away and enticed by his own lust. Then when lust has conceived, it gives birth to sin; and when sin is accomplished, it brings forth death. Do not be deceived, my beloved brethren. Every good thing bestowed and every perfect gift is from above, coming down from the Father of lights, with whom there is no variation, or shifting shadow. In the exercise of His will, He brought us forth by the word of truth, so that we might be, as it were, the first fruits among His creatures. (James 1:13-18)

Since the beginning of time, people have found it easy to blame someone else for their troubles. When God confronted Adam in the Garden of Eden about his sin of disobedience, Adam immediately pointed the finger at his lovely bride, "The woman whom Thou gavest to be with me, she gave me from the tree and I ate." Then when God turned to the woman and asked her to explain herself, she was quick to follow her husband's dubious example by deftly blaming the serpent: "The serpent deceived me and I ate."

Even though Scripture doesn't tell us, I can't help but wonder if Adam and his bride exchanged a sigh of relief (and perhaps a conspiratorial smile) as God proceeded to pronounce a curse on the indicted and convicted serpent. I would love to have seen their faces when He went on to pronounce curses on the two of them as well. I can almost hear them protesting, "But Lord...it wasn't our fault!"

The tendency to blame others for our difficulties reflects the prideful attitude that completely permeates our fallen humanity. Giving in to that temptation on a regular basis is both a mark of spiritual immaturity and a serious sin that God confronts firmly, as the example of Adam and his wife demonstrates.

However, if blaming other people for our problems is a serious sin, blaming God is even more serious. If you read Adam's statement in Genesis 3:12 carefully, you will see a subtle attempt to blame God for his predicament ("...the woman *whom Thou gavest* to be with me..." [emphasis added]). James tells us in vv. 13-15 of chapter one that no one can lay evil at the feet of God, for "God cannot be tempted by evil and He Himself does not tempt anyone." When one of God's sovereignly ordained trials degenerates into a temptation to sin, we have only ourselves to blame.

The word translated "temptation," *peirasmos* in the Greek, has no inherent evil connotation as it does in English. A *peirasmos* can be either an opportunity to glorify God by relying on His strength to endure a trying situation and grow toward maturity; or it can be a temptation to sin by allowing ourselves to be enticed and carried away by our own lust.

Because the Bible is clear about the character of God, we can be sure of one thing—if the trial becomes a temptation, we have only ourselves to blame. God's nature is such that He cannot be tempted by evil, and He Himself does not tempt anyone. Habakkuk 1:13 says in reference to God, "Thine eyes are too pure to approve evil, and Thou canst not look on wickedness with favor." God intends for every trial we encounter to have a beneficial result. When trials result in sin, it is because we choose to heed the call of our human depravity instead of the voice of God.

I am reminded of a story about a slave who worked in the fields of a very cruel master. The cruel master ruled the slave with an iron fist and demanded absolute and complete obedience to his commands. The cruel master was a totally self-centered man who never gave any thought to what was best for the slave.

Imagine the slave's joy when he discovered that the kind and good master who owned the adjoining fields had paid a very high price to buy him away from his cruel master. The kind and good master also demanded absolute and complete obedience from the slave, but he always had the best interests of the slave at heart. Therefore, the slave found it easy to obey his new master out of love and gratitude.

The cruel master hated to see his former slave enjoying his work for the neighbor and would come to the fence between the two fields and command the slave to hop over the fence and perform certain tasks for him. Even though the slave knew he no longer had to obey his former master, he was so accustomed to doing so that he found himself hopping the fence fairly often.

One day as he was working feverishly in his former master's field, feeling guilty and trying to convince himself he really wasn't doing anything wrong, he looked up and saw his new master watching him from the other side of the fence. As their eyes met, the slave was greatly grieved as he remembered that the high price the kind and good master had paid for him was the death of his only son...

That story is not only extremely convicting, it is also an excellent illustration of the truths Paul teaches about salvation in Romans 6. In that chapter Paul explains how our salvation in Jesus Christ breaks the *power* of sin in our lives but leaves our ability to sin intact.

In Romans 6:6 Paul says "that our old self was crucified with Him, that our body of sin might be done away with, that we should no longer be slaves to sin," and in 6:12 he says, "Therefore do not let sin reign in your mortal body that you should obey its lusts." Salvation frees us from sin's bondage so we are, for the first time, able to obey God; however, it does not eliminate our ability to disobey Him. Obedience to God requires us to continually crucify our very real human lusts.

The Christian struggles with sin because his transformed nature's desire to obey God is constantly being challenged by the "lust of the flesh, the lust of the eyes, and the boastful pride of life" (1 John 2:16). Temptation to sin occurs when we allow our minds to dwell on those appealing areas of worldly lust. The longer we look at them, the more appealing they become.

Because I am a small woman who leads a rather sedentary lifestyle, I have to be very careful what I eat if I don't want to become a *large* woman who leads a rather sedentary lifestyle! I have learned not to let my mind dwell on rich, calorie-laden foods. I know from experience that the longer I look at them, the more appealing they become—and the more difficult they are to resist. Whenever I am challenged by tempting treats, I have to discipline my mind to think about something else, or I will soon find I don't fit into my clothes.

The temptation to overeat is just like any other temptation to sin. When we fail to exercise self-control in the power of the Holy Spirit by dwelling on the things of God, we will soon find that lust has conceived and given birth to sin. Dwelling on worldly lusts in our minds is sinful in itself, as are the behaviors that inevitably follow sinful thinking. A young friend of mine used to say, "Your body won't go where your mind hasn't already been." He was right.

The birth of sin brings forth death. Death in the Bible usually signifies some kind of separation. Physical death separates the soul from the body just as spiritual death separates the sinner from God. Unsaved sinners experience judicial separation from God because their unpropitiated[1] sin bars them from His presence. Saved sinners never experience actual separation from God (Romans 8:35-39), but when they fail to confess their sin, the harmony of their familial relationship with Him is disrupted.

There is no remedy for physical death, but spiritual death has been overcome by the resurrection of Jesus Christ. God's judicial forgiveness based on Christ's righteousness imputed to the repentant sinner will restore the judicially separated sinner to Him, just as His ongoing forgiveness of confessing believers restores harmony within the family (1 John 1:9).

Christians must never forget how susceptible they are to temptation. The lure of the world is incredibly strong, and we are most vulnerable when we begin to think we are invincible (1 Corinthians 10:12). The only protection we have against the enticements of sin is the power of the Holy Spirit in us. When we allow our minds to be lured away from the things of God to the things of the world, we are asking for trouble.

Not only are we more likely to sin when we tune in to the world, but we are also more likely to accuse God of tempting us. The world does not understand God's purpose for trials and maligns His goodness by attributing evil intentions to Him. When Christians allow themselves to be deceived by the world's lies, they not only fail to reap the greatest benefit from the trial but also lose a valuable opportunity to glorify God by demonstrating the sufficiency of His power and grace to endure difficulties.

Because God is good, He loves us perfectly. As we learn to understand and trust this aspect of His character, we begin to see trials as one of the good and perfect gifts that come down from the Father of lights with whom there is no variation, or shifting shadow.

God knows each of His children better than they know themselves. He created them, transformed them and gifted them to do specialized work in the building of His Kingdom. He knows exactly what each one of us needs to become all that He wants us to be, and He sovereignly controls every circumstance of our lives to accomplish His purposes for us. Even when an enemy intentionally works to bring evil against us, God will use his evil intent to produce a good result

(Genesis 50:20; Romans 8:28-29). When God is for us, no one can effectively stand against us (Romans 8:31).

Trials help us mature in our faith because they teach us to rely on God's perfect love and power even if we don't understand the purpose behind the trial. When my daughter was very young, she fell against a display rack in a store and suffered a jagged puncture wound in the soft tissue of her side. We cleaned and bandaged the wound immediately, but within a week, it began to show signs of infection.

She was too young to understand why I took her to the doctor and held her down on the examining table while he cleaned and disinfected the wound. All she really understood was I was helping him to hurt her. At that moment she could have been easily persuaded that I didn't love her at all since she was much too young to understand the depth of love it took to hold her on the table. You see, I knew what would happen if I didn't require her to endure a trial she didn't want to endure.

As she has grown and matured, she has developed a greater appreciation for the potential benefits of painful situations and for people who love her enough to "hold her down." It has been very gratifying for me in the past few years to see her begin to learn the value of trials.

We need to remember that God does not enjoy putting us through trials. The truth is He loves us too much to allow us to escape them. He knows the beneficial outcome of endurance and He desires the glorious testimony of our confident trust.

The key to trusting God in the midst of trials is remembering that He sovereignly ordains our circumstances for His glory and for our benefit. When we keep that truth before us, we can begin to understand what James is saying—that everything God ordains, even trials, come to us as good and perfect gifts from the Father who loves us perfectly.

Verse 18 tells us that only as transformed believers in Jesus Christ can we understand these truths. God has "brought us forth by the word of truth," and given us new life in Him. The indwelling Holy Spirit who illumines our understanding of God's truth is able to keep us from deception, as long as we commit ourselves to learning from Him.

James reminds the readers of his day that they were the first fruits—the promise of a rich harvest to come. Twentieth-century believers are part of that promised harvest, and as such we are responsible to draw on the life within us to respond to trials in a way that honors God by establishing a pattern of righteousness in our lives.

---

[1] Propitiation refers to the sacrificial death of Christ on the cross that satisfied God's wrath against sin so He could extend forgiveness to His elect.

Review Questions

1. How did Adam and his wife respond when God confronted them about their sin? How does their response relate to what James says in James 1:13-15?

2. Explain how a *peirasmos* can be either an opportunity to glorify God or a temptation to sin.

3. What does Romans 6 teach about our struggle with sin?

4. How does 1 John 2:16 describe temptation? Can you give some examples of each type of temptation?

5. Describe the process expressed in James 1:15. Use examples from "real life" to illustrate your description if you can.

6. Explain how trials can be understood to be among the good and perfect gifts coming down from the Father of lights.

Applying the Word

1. Describe a time in your life when you succumbed to a
   temptation to sin. On this particular occasion, how were you
   enticed and carried away by your own lust? How did you
   respond to the lust of your flesh, the lust of our eyes, and/or
   the boastful pride of life? What did uncontrolled lust con-
   ceive in your heart and mind? Describe the sin that was born
   from that conception. What kind of death did you experience
   as a result of your sin? Have you repented and confessed
   this sin?

2. Write an explanation of the lust-to-death process described in James 1:15 that you could use to teach this concept to a young child. Now write an explanation of the same process that you could use to teach this concept to a teenager.

Digging Deeper

1. Study Romans 5-8. Feel free to use any good biblical reference books available to you and to consult reputable commentaries. When you have completed your study, write a clear, concise explanation of what Paul means when he says Christians have been "freed from sin." (Romans 6:7)

2. Study the book of Job. Did Job ever fully understand the reasons behind the trials he endured? How did God respond to Job when Job sought the reasons behind his trials? Explain how the trials of Job could be seen as good and perfect gifts coming down from the Father of lights.

"Peace, contentment and joy in the Christian life result from faithfully pursuing the purpose for which we were created."

Chapter Seven

Time to Get to Work!

---

*This you know, my beloved brethren. But let everyone
be quick to hear, slow to speak, and slow to anger; for
the anger of man does not achieve the righteousness of
God. Therefore putting aside all filthiness and all that
remains of wickedness, in humility receive the word implanted, which is able to save your souls. But prove your-
selves doers of the word, and not merely hearers who
delude themselves. For if anyone is a hearer of the word
and not a doer, he is like a man who looks at his natural
face in a mirror; for once he has looked at himself and
gone away, he has immediately forgotten what kind of
person he was. But one who looks intently at the perfect
law, the law of liberty, and abides by it, not having become a forgetful hearer, but an effectual doer, this man
shall be blessed in what he does. (James 1:19-25)*

One of the most consistent and pervasive themes of
the Bible is the call for believers to pursue righteousness in
all that they do. (Matthew 6:33; 1 Timothy 6:11; 2 Timothy
2:22; 3:16-17; 1 Peter 2:24; 1 John 2:29; 1 John 3:10) Believers
cannot glorify God and enjoy their relationship with Him

unless they are seeking to reflect the righteousness that is inherent in the nature of God.

Ephesians 2:10 reminds us that we were created to do good works, and Matthew 5:16 tells us that the good works we do glorify God. John 14:27, 15:11, and 16:33 are representative of the many verses in the Bible that teach us that peace, contentment and joy in the Christian life result from faithfully pursuing the purpose for which we were created.

Unfortunately, pursuing righteousness doesn't come naturally to any of us. (Perhaps that's why Scripture reminds us of it so often!) Because we retain our proclivity to sin after we are transformed in Jesus Christ, we must *pursue* righteousness in order to obtain it. When we cease to make the effort to develop righteousness, we default to our natural sinful inclinations.

If you have any doubts that your natural inclinations are sinful rather than righteous, consider (honestly now!) how you would respond in certain questionable situations if you were absolutely sure you would never get caught or no one would ever know what you did. Someone has accurately stated that character is what you do when no one is looking.

Perhaps the most difficult time for any of us to pursue righteousness is when we are facing trials. James understands that we are quite likely to become angry during trying times and that *the anger of man does not achieve the righteousness of God.* Avoiding anger in order to pursue righteousness in the midst of a trial involves listening to God, controlling our speech, receiving the word of God implanted, and doing what He says.

Verse 19 says we must be quick to hear, slow to speak and slow to anger. We cannot pursue righteousness in a trial until we are willing to listen carefully to God's truth regarding both the purpose of the trial and the way He wants us to respond to it. Thus, the first step in dealing with a trial is to seek God's wisdom through prayerful study of His Word.

Secondly, we must be slow to speak. Human beings have a compulsive desire to talk about their difficulties—to anyone who will listen for as long as they will listen. We talk to friends, parents, spouses, pastors, store clerks, bartenders... We complain, we fret, we speculate, we threaten, we moan, we "vent." It's interesting that "counseling" is often referred to as *talk-therapy*. How often have you heard, "Oh, he just needed someone to listen to him talk about his problem."? How often have you thanked someone for "just listening"?

James says, "When you have a problem, be *slow to speak*. Don't run all over town talking about your problem. Close your mouth and listen to God."

Being quick to hear and slow to speak is a very difficult assignment for fallen human beings; however, *transformed* fallen human beings can do it. The indwelling Holy Spirit is always ready to help us seek God's wisdom so we can develop a righteous attitude toward the trial and respond to it with righteous behavior. When we remember to lean on His enabling power, we are less likely to become angry about the trial and respond unrighteously

When we respond to a trial in anger—either against God or against our fellow man, we short-circuit God's intended purpose for the trial. The anger of man does not produce the righteousness of God. When we allow anger to control our response to a trial, we hinder the development of righteousness in our lives, we do not glorify God, and we stifle our own joy.

Accomplishing God's purposes in a trial involves more than closing our mouths and listening to God, however. It also involves *doing* what we hear Him say. God's written word tells us everything we need to know to live in a manner that pleases Him (Psalm 19:7-14; 2 Timothy 3:15-17; 2 Peter 1:3-4). We cannot listen to God if we ignore His written revelation. But, even a thorough knowledge of God's Word will not get us through a trial righteously unless we put that knowledge into practice. This is why James tells us to receive the Word implanted.

God's Word implanted will grow and bear fruit under the right conditions. If you have ever done any gardening, you know that sticking a seed in the ground and covering it with dirt doesn't guarantee growth and fruitfulness. If you want your seed to grow, you must stimulate its growth by watering it, fertilizing it, keeping it in the sun, and perhaps supporting it with stakes or wires. You must also eliminate hindrances to its growth by protecting it from things like pounding hail storms, unexpected frosts, and dastardly predators (such as bugs, worms, and the next door neighbor's dog!)

God's Word implanted in our hearts must be cultivated in much the same way. We stimulate its growth by establishing routine habits of worship, prayer, study, fellowship, and righteous behavior. We eliminate hindrances to its growth by putting aside all filthiness and all that remains of wickedness, that is, by avoiding and resisting temptation, examining our hearts regularly and confessing all known sin.

Christians in our society are growing increasingly insensitive to sin and its devastating effects on their lives.[1] One of the reasons behind this trend is the Church's infatuation with the self-esteem teachings of modern psychology. As we become more and more focused on esteeming, exalting, satisfying, and fulfilling *ourselves*, we become less focused on glorifying God. As we increase, He decreases.

Our increasing self-centeredness encourages us to justify, excuse, or ignore our sin because recognizing and confessing sin does nothing to enhance our self-image. What we have forgotten in this tragic shift of focus is that sin is an abomination to God, and that the Christian's purpose in life is to glorify God—not exalt himself. We must be more concerned with what sin does to our relationship with God than we are with what acknowledging our sin will do to our pride.

Another unfortunate outcome of the church's growing infatuation with "selfism" is an increasing reluctance to accept and endure trials as an important and necessary element of our maturity in Christ. The Theology of Self-Esteem exalts a "god of love" who wants us to feel good about ourselves and doesn't want us to suffer. Trials and difficulties are presented as devices of the devil sent to destroy our confidence in ourselves and in our "loving god."

The proper Christian response to trials, according to this line of thinking, is to avoid them, escape them or "take authority over them" even if we have to disobey God's written Word to do it. I cringe every time I hear a Christian say something like, "I know what the Bible says about divorce, but I also know God doesn't want me to be this miserable." God's primary concern is our holiness—not our happiness (Titus 2:11-14). As a matter of fact, the only way a true child of God can know full joy in life (which far surpasses human happiness) is to pursue holiness.[2]

Trials play a vital part in developing a holy and righteous lifestyle, and should be considered all joy because of their potential to mature us and glorify God. In order for that potential to be realized, we must listen to God, eliminate known sin from our lives, and then practice doing the Word. James tells us to examine the Scriptures intently, as if we were examining our own faces in a mirror, and then do something about what we see.

I don't know about you, but when I examine my face intently in a mirror, I am usually trying to repair or conceal the ravages of time. Once I have determined what needs to be done, I must remain in front of the mirror and allow it to guide me while I work to remedy the situation. I can't fix my face by looking away from the mirror to the wall. In the same way, I can't implement godly conduct in a trial by looking away from Scripture to the world. I need to know God's Word and do what it says regardless of what the secular experts say.

When we deal with trials by listening to God and acting on His Word, His purposes will be accomplished, and we will be blessed in all we do. Knowing this, we can certainly consider it all joy when we encounter various trials.

---

[1] For an excellent analysis of and solution to this problem, see John MacArthur Jr., *The Vanishing Conscience.* Dallas: Word Publishing, 1994.

[2] For more information about pursuing holiness, see Jerry Bridges, *The Pursuit of Holiness.* Colorado Springs: Navpress, 1978.

Review Questions

1. How does being quick to hear and slow to speak help us respond to trials in a manner that glorifies God?

2. How does being quick to hear and slow to speak inhibit our natural tendency to become angry about trials?

3. How does the Holy Spirit help us listen to God during a trial?

4. What kinds of habits encourage the growth of the implanted word in our hearts? What kinds of actions hinder that growth? Explain how these habits encourage and hinder that growth.

5. Explain how exalting self interferes with glorifying God.

6. Explain the mirror analogy James uses in chapter 1, verses 23-25.

Applying the Word

1. For a period of one month, make a point of seeking God's wisdom through Bible study and prayer *before* you talk to another person about difficulties or trials. If this is a new practice for you, record how this practice changes your attitude and behavior during trials.

2. For a period of one month, keep a record of your responses to trials. Record each trial you face during the month, including the date, time of day, and a description of the circumstances. Also record detailed descriptions of your initial and long-term responses to the trial. At the end of the month, evaluate your responses. Do you typically respond in anger to trials? Do you tend to talk too much about your trials? Do you habitually listen to God during a trial? Do you need to confess any sin associated with your response to these trials? Do you need to repair any relationships with people? What changes do you need to make in the way you respond to trials? How will you go about making these changes?

Digging Deeper

1. Using a concordance and any other reliable study tools available to you, do a study on biblical commands regarding the call to pursue righteousness in our lives. Based on your study of James 1, explain how the anger of man impacts our response to this call.

2. Based on your study of James 1, explain how the anger of man impacts our response to this call to pursue righteousness in our lives.

"We should not wait until we are reeling from another of the world's blows to start thinking about how to handle the situation."

Chapter Eight

Be Prepared

Not long after we were married, my husband bought a little plaque for me to hang over my desk that read, LORD, GRANT ME PATIENCE... AND I WANT IT RIGHT NOW! I was amazed at how well he had gotten to know me in such a short time. I enjoyed that little plaque until a friend reminded me that patience comes through tribulation (Romans 5:3-5). Then I began wonder if I should quit praying for patience!

Fortunately, God does not leave decisions like these up to me. Galatians 5:22-23 tells us that patience is one element of the nine-fold fruit of the Spirit, and Romans 8:9 leaves no doubt that all Christians possess the indwelling Holy Spirit. Therefore, as a believer in Jesus Christ, my life will reflect the fruit of that indwelling Spirit to some degree.

Developing that fruit into full flower is a joint effort between God and me. Philippians 2:12-13 says, "So then, my beloved, just as you have always obeyed, not as in my presence only, but now much more in my absence, work out your salvation with fear and trembling; for it is God who is at work in you, both to will and to work for His good pleasure."

God sovereignly ordains the circumstances of my life to make sure I have plenty of opportunities to cultivate and nourish the the fruit of the Spirit, and He gives me the Spirit's power to enable me to respond to those circumstances in ways that will accomplish His purposes. My responsibility is to stay alert to those opportunities and make every effort to respond to them righteously.

Among those sovereignly ordained opportunities to develop the fruit of the Spirit (particularly patience) are the trials we encounter in this fallen world. The first chapter of James has given us some valuable guidance regarding our response to trials, but before we leave this subject, we need to consider one final issue—preparing to face trials.

One of the women I know is an attorney who works very hard to prepare her "trial strategy" before she goes into court. She prepares carefully *before* she walks into the courtroom so she will be ready to deal with a wide variety of contingencies. She doesn't wait until she hears the opposing attorney's arguments to begin preparing her case. She doesn't always use everything she has prepared, but she is rarely caught off guard.

We need to prepare for trials the same way she does. We should not wait until we are reeling from another of the world's blows to start thinking about how to handle the situation. We need to prepare ourselves *beforehand*. Another little plaque that hangs over my desk illustrates this principle very well. It looks like this:

PLAN AHE
A
D

That little plaque is instructive as well as amusing because it illustrates so clearly what happens when we fail to heed the advice it gives.

A helpful "trial strategy" for Christians who want to glorify God and enjoy Him forever should include the following elements. Remember, however, that God deals with His children as individuals, so you should consider expanding or adapting this outline to fit your particular situation.

First of all, *expect* to encounter trials in your life. First Peter 4:12 says, "Beloved, do not be surprised at the fiery ordeal among you, which comes upon you for your testing, as though some strange thing were happening to you." Trials are an essential part of Christian maturity, and should not surprise us.

Second, take full advantage of the non-trying times in your life to learn all you can from God's Word about facing trials. I often tell people the best time to give someone a copy of *James on Trials* is not when they are in the midst of struggling with a major calamity. Most of us find it very difficult to concentrate on learning new skills when we are distraught. We also tend to be somewhat less than receptive to those who encourage us to "change our attitudes" when we are physically or emotionally distressed. You will learn God's principles for facing trials much more effectively if you study them *before* you need to put them into practice.

Third, maintain regular habits of Bible study, prayer, and attention to godly preaching and teaching. The more you expose yourself to the truths of God, the better prepared you will be to face the routine demands of living as well as major difficulties.

Fourth, develop a support system. Cultivate deep spiritual friendships and discipling relationships. Cherish people who love you enough to hold you accountable to God's truth and to respond appropriately when you need help. I have a friend I don't see very often because we live in different cities. However, we work at cherishing our relationship because we trust each other. I can call her when I am struggling with a trial and know she will gently remind me of the biblical truths she knows I already know. (I also know she will split the phone bill with me.)

Finally, pray for opportunities to grow in your faith. This is a difficult prayer for most of us because growth can be so very painful; however, praying for these opportunities becomes easier when we heed the words of James and "consider it all joy, my brethren, when you encounter various trials."

Review Questions

1. Explain what Galatians 5:22-23 and Romans 5:3-5 teach about patience. (Some translations use the word "endurance" instead of patience.)

2. Explain what Paul is teaching in Philippians 2:12-13 in your own words, and indicate how this teaching should affect the way we understand and respond to trials

3. Why is it important to "plan ahead" to handle trials?

4. List the steps in the "trial strategy" recommended in this chapter. Can you think of any other steps that would be helpful to include in this strategy?

Applying the Word

1. Describe a specific trial you are facing now or have faced recently. Make a detailed plan for dealing with this trial using the principles you have learned in this study. Share your plan with someone who loves you enough to hold you accountable to God's truths in carrying out your plan.

2. How would you expand or adapt the "trial strategy" recommended in this chapter to make it more useful to you as an individual?

3. What have you learned from this study that will help you mature in your faith so you can glorify God and enjoy your relationship with Him more effectively?

Digging Deeper

1. Study the subject of patience (endurance, longsuffering, perseverance) in the Bible and write an explanation of why "patience comes through tribulation." Do you think a person can develop the quality of patience without encountering tribulation. Why or why not?

Recommended Reading

Jay Adams, *A Thirst for Wholeness*. Wheaton, IL: Victor Books, 1988.

Jay Adams, *The Grand Demonstration: A Biblical Study of the So-Called Problem of Evil*. Santa Barbara, CA: EastGate Publishers, 1991.

Jerry Bridges, *The Pursuit of Holiness*. Colorado Springs: Navpress, 1978.

Jerry Bridges, *The Practice of Godliness*. Colorado Springs: Navpress, 1983.

D. Edmond Hiebert, *James*. Chicago: Moody Press, 1979, 1992. (original title: *The Epistle of James*).

Michael Horton, *Made in America: The Shaping of Modern American Evangelicalism*. Grand Rapids: Baker Books, 1991.

John F. MacArthur, Jr., *Faith Works: The Gospel According to the Apostles*. Dallas: Word Publishing, 1993.

John F. MacArthur, Jr., *The Vanishing Conscience*. Dallas: Word Publishing Company, 1994.

Edith Schaeffer, *Affliction*. Old Tappan, NJ: Fleming H. Revell Company, 1978.

A. W. Tozer, *The Pursuit of God*. Camp Hill, PA: Christian Publications, Inc., 1982.

Appendix A

What Must I Do to be Saved?

A strange sound drifted through the Philippian Jail as midnight approached. The sound of human voices—but not the expected groans of the two men who had earlier been beaten with rods and fastened in stocks. Rather, the peaceful singing of praises to their God.

While the other prisoners quietly listened to them, the jailer dozed off, content with the bizarre calm generated by these two preachers, who, hours before, had stirred so much commotion in the city.

Suddenly a deafening roar filled the prison, and the ground began to shake violently. Sturdy doors convulsed and popped open. Chains snapped and fell at prisoners' feet. Startled into full wakefulness, the jailer stared, horrified, at the wide-open doors that guaranteed his prisoners' escape— and his own death. Under Roman law, jailers paid with their lives when prisoners escaped. Resolutely, he drew his sword, thinking it better to die by his own hand than by Roman execution.

"Stop! Don't harm yourself—we are all here!", a voice boomed from the darkened inner cell. The jailer called for lights and was astonished to discover his prisoners standing quietly amid their broken chains. Trembling with fear, he rushed in and fell at the feet of the two preachers. As soon as he was able, he led them out of the ruined prison and asked in utter astonishment, "Sirs, What must I do to be saved?"

In the entire history of the world, no one has ever asked a more important question. The jailer's words that day may well have been motivated by his critical physical need, but the response of Paul and Silas addressed his even more critical spiritual need: "Believe in the Lord Jesus, and you shall be saved, you and your household."[1]

If you have never "believed in the Lord Jesus," your spiritual need, just like the jailer's, is critical. As long as your life is stained with sin, God cannot receive you into His presence. The Bible says that sin has placed a separation between you and God (Isaiah 59:2). It goes on to say that your nature has been so permeated by sin that you no longer have any desire to serve and obey God (Romans 3:10-12); therefore, you are not likely to recognize or care that a separation exists. Your situation is truly desperate because those who are separated from God will spend eternity in hell.

Since your sinful nature is unresponsive to God, the only way you can be saved from your desperate situation is for God to take the initiative. And this He has done! Even though all men and women deserve the punishment of hell because of their sin, God's love has prompted Him to save some who will serve Him in obedience. He did this by sending His Son, the Lord Jesus Christ, to remove the barrier of sin between God and His chosen ones (Colossians 2:13-14).

What is there about Jesus that enables Him to do this? First of all, He is God. While He was on earth He said, "He who has seen Me has seen the Father," (John 14:9) and "I and the Father are one." (John 10:30) Because He said these things, you must conclude one of three things about His true identity: (1) He was a lunatic who believed he was God when he really wasn't; (2) He was a liar who was willing to die a hideous death for what he knew was a lie; or (3) His words are true and He is God.

Lunatics don't live the way Jesus did, and liars don't die the way He did, so if the Bible's account of Jesus' life and words is true, you can be sure He *is* God.

Since Jesus is God, He is perfectly righteous and holy. God's perfect righteousness and holiness demands that sin be punished (Ezekiel 18:4), and Jesus' perfect righteousness and holiness qualified Him to bear the punishment for the sins of those who will be saved (Romans 6:23). Jesus is the only person who never committed a sin; therefore, the punishment He bore when He died on the cross could be accepted by God as satisfaction of His justice in regard to the sins of others.

If someone you love commits a crime and is sentenced to die, you may offer to die in his place. However, if you have also committed crimes worthy of death, your death cannot satisfy the law's demands for your crimes *and* your loved one's. You can only die in his place if you are innocent of any wrongdoing.

Since Jesus lived a perfect life, God's justice could be satisfied by allowing Him to die for the sins of those who will be saved. Because God is perfectly righteous and holy, He could not act in love at the expense of justice. By sending

Jesus to die, God demonstrated His love *by acting to satisfy His own justice.* (Romans 3:26)

Jesus did more than die, however. He also rose from the dead. By raising Jesus from the dead, God declared that He had accepted Jesus' death in the place of those who will be saved. Because Jesus lives eternally with God, those for whom Jesus died can be assured they will also spend eternity in heaven (John 14:1-3). The separation of sin has been removed!

Ah, but the all-important question remains unanswered: What must *you do* to be saved? If God has sent His Son into the world for sinners, and Jesus Christ died in their place, what is left for you to do? You must respond in faith to what God has done. This is what Paul meant when he told the jailer, "Believe in the Lord Jesus, and you shall be saved."

Believing in the Lord Jesus demands three responses from you: (1) An understanding of the facts regarding your hopeless sinful condition and God's action to remove the sin barrier that separates you from Him; (2) acceptance of those facts as true and applicable to you; and (3) a willingness to trust and depend upon God to save you from sin. This involves willingly placing yourself under His authority and acknowledging His sovereign right to rule over you.

But, you say, how can I do this if sin has eliminated my ability to know and appreciate God's work on my behalf? Rest assured that if you desire to have the sin barrier that separates you from God removed, He is already working to change your natural inability to respond. He is extending His gracious offer of salvation to you and will give you the faith to receive it.

If you believe God is working to call you to Himself, read the words He has written to you in the Bible (begin with the book of John in the New Testament) and pray that His Holy Spirit will help you understand what is written there. Continue to read and pray until you are ready to *repent*, that is, to turn away from sin and commit yourself to serving God.

Is there any other way you can be saved? God Himself says no, there is not. The Bible He wrote says that Jesus is the only way the sin barrier between you and God can be removed (John 14:6; Acts 4:12). He is your hope, and He is your *only* hope.

If you have questions or need any help in this matter, please write to The Evangelism Team, Providence Presbyterian Church, P. O. Box 14651, Albuquerque, NM 87191, before the day is over. God has said in His Bible that a day of judgment is coming, and after that day no one will be saved (Acts 17:30-31; 2 Thessalonians 1:7-9). The time to act is now.

---

[1] For a full biblical account of this event, see Acts 16:11-40.

Appendix B

What is the Reformed Faith?

"The Reformed Faith"[1] can be defined as a theology that describes and explains the sovereign God's revelation of His actions in history to glorify Himself by redeeming selected men and women from the just consequences of their self-inflicted depravity.

It is first and foremost *theology* (the study of God), not *anthropology* (the study of man). Reformed thinking concentrates on developing a true knowledge of God that serves as the necessary context for all other knowledge. It affirms that the created world, including humanity itself, cannot be accurately understood apart from its relationship with the Creator.

The Reformed Faith describes and explains God's revelation of Himself and His actions to humanity; it does not consist of people's attempts to define God as they wish. The Reformed Faith asserts that God has revealed Himself in two distinct ways. He reveals His existence, wisdom and power through the created universe—a process known as *natural revelation* (Romans 1:18-32); and He reveals His requirements and plans for mankind through His written Word, the Bible—a process known as *special revelation* (2 Timothy 3:16-17).

Reformed theologians uphold the Bible as the inspired, infallible, inerrant, authoritative, and fully sufficient communication of truth from God to us. When they say the Bible is "inspired," they mean that the Bible was actually written by God through the agency of human authorship in a miraculous way that preserved the thoughts of God from the taint of human sinfulness (2 Peter 1:20-21).

When they say the Bible is infallible, they mean it is *incapable* of error, and when they say it is inerrant, they mean the Bible, *in actual fact*, contains no errors. The Bible is authoritative because it comes from God whose authority over His creation is absolute (Isaiah 46:9-10). And it is completely sufficient because it contains everything necessary for us to know and live according to God's requirements (2 Peter 1:3-4).

By studying God's revelation of Himself and His work, Reformed theologians have learned two foundational truths that structure their thinking about God's relationship with human beings: God is absolutely sovereign, and people are totally depraved.[2]

Reformed thought affirms that God, by definition, is absolutely sovereign—that is, He controls and superintends every circumstance of life either by direct miraculous intervention or by the ordinary outworking of His providence. Reformed theologians understand that a "god" who is not sovereign cannot be God because his power would not be absolute. Since the Reformed Faith accepts the Bible's teaching regarding the sovereignty of God, it denies that *anything* occurs outside of God's control.

The Reformed faith affirms the biblical teaching that Adam was created with the ability to sin and chose to do so by disobeying a clear command of God (Genesis 3:1-7).

Choosing to sin changed basic human nature and left us unable not to sin—or *totally depraved.* Total depravity does not mean that all people are as bad as they possibly could be, but that every facet of their character is tainted with sin, leaving them incapable and undesirous of fellowship with God. The Reformed faith denies that totally depraved men and women have any ability to seek after or submit to God of their own free will. Left to themselves, totally depraved men and women will remain out of fellowship with God for all eternity.

The only way for any of these men and women to have their fellowship with God restored is for God Himself to take the initiative. And the Bible declares that He has graciously chosen to do so (John 14:16). *For His own glory,* He has chosen some of those depraved men and women to live in fellowship with Him. His choice is determined by His own good pleasure and not by any virtue in the ones He has chosen. For this reason, *grace* is defined in Reformed thought as "unmerited favor."

God accomplished the salvation of His chosen ones by sending His Son, the Lord Jesus Christ, to bear God's righteous wrath against sin so He could forgive those He had chosen. Even though Christ's work was perfect and complete, its effectiveness is limited to those who are chosen by God for salvation. Christ would not have been required to suffer any more or any less had a different number been chosen for redemption, but the benefit of His suffering is applied only to those who are called by God to believe in Him.

All of those who are thus effectually called by God will eventually believe and be saved, even though they may resist for a time (John 6:37). They cannot forfeit the salvation they have received (John 10:27-30; Romans 8:31-39).

Reformed thought affirms the clear teaching of the Bible that salvation is by faith alone through Christ alone (John 14:6; Acts 4:12; Ephesians 2:8-9), and that human works play no part in salvation although they are generated by it (Ephesians 2:10). Salvation transforms a person's nature, giving him or her the ability and the desire to serve and obey God. The unresponsive heart of stone is changed into a sensitive heart of flesh that responds readily to God's voice (Ezekiel 36:25-27) and desires to glorify Him out of gratitude for the indescribable gift of salvation.

Reformed thought affirms that *God works in history to redeem* His chosen ones through a series of covenants. These covenants define His Law, assess penalties for breaking His Law, and provide for the imputation of Jesus' vicarious fulfillment of God's requirements to those God intends to redeem.[3]

The Reformed faith affirms that we were created and exist solely to glorify God, and denies that God exists to serve us. It affirms that God acts to glorify Himself by putting His attributes on display, and that His self-glorifying actions are thoroughly righteous since He is the only Being in creation worthy of glorification. It denies that God is *primarily* motivated to act by man's needs, but affirms that all of God's actions are motivated *primarily* for His own glory.

The Reformed faith emerged as a distinct belief system during the Sixteenth and Seventeenth Centuries when men like Luther, Calvin, Zwingli, and Knox fought against the Roman Catholic Church to restore Christian doctrine to biblical truth. These men were labeled "Reformers," but they would have been better labeled "Restorers" since their goal was to correct abuses and distortions of Christianity that were rampant in the established Roman church. Reformed thinkers since their day have sought to align their understanding of God and His actions in history as closely as possible to His revealed truth.

[1] This brief overview of basic Reformed beliefs is not intended to be a full explanation of or apologetic for the Reformed Faith. For a more detailed description and analysis of the Reformed Faith see: R.C. Sproul, *Grace Unknown* (Grand Rapids: Baker Books, 1997), Loraine Boettner, *The Reformed Faith* (Phillipsburg, N.J.: Presbyterian and Reformed, 1983), *Back to Basics: Rediscovering the Richness of the Reformed Faith,* ed. David G. Hagopian (Phillipsburg, N.J.: P & R Publishing, 1996), *The Westminster Confession of Faith* (with its accompanying Catechisms), or the theological writings of John Calvin, B. B. Warfield, Charles Hodge, and Louis Berkhof.

[2] Both of these truths are taught throughout the pages of Scripture; however, the sovereignty of God can be seen very clearly in Isaiah 40-60 and in Job 38-42, while the total depravity of man is described quite graphically in Romans 3:10-18.

[3] An excellent discussion of these covenants is contained in chapter 5 of R. C. Sproul, *Grace Unknown.*

The Purpose of Deo Volente Publishing

"And do not be conformed to this world,
but be transformed by the renewing of your mind,
that you may prove what is that good and
acceptable and perfect will of God"
Romans 12:2 (NKJV)

Deo Volente Publishing exists to help make the exhortation of Romans 12:2 a living, daily reality in the believer's life.

Our goal is:
- to edify believers in Christ,
- to encourage non-conformity to the world's standards,
- to exhort believers to live radically transformed lives that reflect the knowledge, enjoyment and practice of what is good, acceptable, and perfect in God's sight.

We will endeavor to meet our goal by publishing material that:
- is consistently Reformed in theology,
- is intensely practical for a daily Christian walk,
- and encourages holy living in every aspect of life through the reforming power of God's Word.

DEO VOLENTE PUBLISHING
P.O. BOX 4847
LOS ALAMOS, NM 87544